Graduate...
Prayers,
Promises &
inspiration
for the Road Ahead

Reminders that God is with you all along the way

Inspired by Faith

Graduate...Prayers, Promises & inspiration for the Road Ahead
©Product Concept Mfg., Inc.

Graduate...Prayers, Promises & inspiration for the Road Ahead
ISBN 978-0-9886719-3-5

Published by Product Concept Mfg., Inc.
2175 N. Academy Circle #200, Colorado Springs, CO 80909

©2015 Product Concept Mfg., Inc. All rights reserved.

Written and Compiled by Patricia Mitchell, Vick J. Kuyper
in association with Product Concept Mfg., Inc.

All scripture quotations are from the King James version
of the Bible unless otherwise noted.

Scriptures taken from the Holy Bible,
New International Version®, NIV®.
Copyright © 1973, 1978, 1984 by Biblica, Inc.™
Used by permission of Zondervan.
All rights reserved worldwide.
www.zondervan.com

Sayings not having a credit listed are contributed by writers
for Product Concept Mfg., Inc. or in a rare case,
the author is unknown.

Graduate...
Prayers, Promises, &
inspiration
for the Road Ahead

LET YOUR
LIGHT SO SHINE...

MATTHEW 5:16

The important thing is not to stop questioning.

~Albert Einstein

You're ready to start an exciting new chapter in your life. Adventures, opportunities, and discoveries are waiting for you, as well as good times with friends, both old and new.

Yes, you will face challenges, but you have what it takes to not only overcome them, but learn from them and grow stronger because of them. You might surprise yourself, but others know you have everything you need within you.

Whatever direction you take and wherever you go, God is right beside you. When you need a reminder of His presence, or a little encouragement in your day, turn to one of the short reflections in this book.

May God bless you richly in the days and years ahead, and may you enjoy to the fullest all the wonderful things He has in store for you!

It's Your Story!

Each and every day, you're writing a story that's never been told before. You're thinking thoughts, building relationships, meeting challenges and seeing the world in a way no one else has ever done or will ever do again. Both your path and your perspective are one-of-a-kind. So are the unique contributions you'll make to this world.

Even before you were born, God began writing a few details of your story. When and where you'd enter the world. What family you'd become part of. The color of your eyes, your hair, your skin. Your individual gifts and abilities.... But how you weave details such as these into the larger epic of your life is up to you.

Throughout your life, you'll undoubtedly encounter circumstances beyond your control. But the real story—your story—isn't what

6

happens to you, but what you do with what happens. What some people label adversity others view as opportunity. How about you? You choose the final storyline, how you react in any given situation, what you say and what you do.

God created you and He is fully aware of your amazing potential. He's cheering you on to write yourself into a role that fits who you were created to be: a hero with heart. You don't need a cape and a pair of tights to lead a storybook life. You've got what it takes to live in a way that reflects your true identity. Go ahead and choose to do the "write" thing.

Do not go where the path may lead, go instead where there is no path and leave a trail.
Ralph Waldo Emerson

THE COMPASS WITHIN

Before you were born, God gave you a very special gift: your own personal compass. He built it right into your brain, so you don't have to worry about losing it or leaving it behind on the nightstand when you head out to face the day. God designed this internal compass— your conscience—to help guide you safely through life.

A handheld compass aligns with the magnetic north pole. The compass in your head aligns with God's heart. It helps you weigh your choices in light of God's perspective. That way, when you come to a figurative fork in the road you'll know the wisest way to go.

The number of choices you face each day can be overwhelming. Paper or plastic. Poco or Mucho Cappuccino Supremo. Your conscience doesn't need to help guide you through decisions like these. All you need is common sense. It's the choices with consequences, sometimes life-changing ones, that require careful consideration and heartfelt prayer...Should I accept this job? Should I continue in this relationship? Should I speak up or hold my tongue?

Use the compass God's given you. It will help you navigate your way toward a better life.

A "hunch" just might be God trying to get your attention.

THE REAL SECRET TO SUCCESS

If you're surfing the web for the secret to success, you'll find many articles on tips, tricks or "Ten Easy Steps" that they promise will help you achieve your goals. But God has a better plan, no tricks involved.

God's secret to success is simple. He doesn't expect absolute perfection; in fact, He offers you the freedom to fail. Granted, failure doesn't sound as inviting as Ten Easy Steps. But if you're not afraid of messing things up once in awhile, you'll risk more. You'll push yourself further. You'll try again.

God doesn't expect absolute perfection from you. If He did, why would He place such a high value on forgiveness and grace?

So, go ahead and put everything you've got into what you're trying to accomplish. Do your very best. But if it ends in less than success, don't beat yourself up. Learn something. Figure out what you could improve on. Then, pick yourself up, dust off your pride and try again. Either you'll steadily work your way toward achieving your goal or you'll come to the realization that it's time to drop this dream and head in a new direction.

Whether you to want to travel abroad, help endangered species, or apply to your dream college—whatever your goal—don't be afraid to step out and try. When you succeed, celebrate! When you fail, fail forward. Failing doesn't make you a failure. It makes you a person with the guts to try. That's true success.

**Big shots are only little shots
who keep shooting.**
Christopher Morley

11

Free To Soar

Ever try to walk an energetic puppy? Chances are, he walked you! That little guy, so eager to explore the world, dragged you along as he tugged and pulled at the leash. But you didn't let go, did you? Because if you did, that dog would take off like an Olympic sprinter!

A lot of people have something in common with that tugging, pulling puppy. They yearn to explore the opportunities all around them, but they feel reined in, restricted, constrained, as if they were on a leash. Sometimes that "leash" is fear of doing something outside their comfort zone, going beyond their sphere of familiarity. They might be chained by personal addictions or unhealthy habits, which limit their ability to take advantage of real possibilities. Maybe negative self-talk, low expectations, or lack of motivation keeps them leash-bound.

Have you ever felt reined in by a self-made leash? What is it? What's the leash that holds you back from going as far as God created you to go?

Unlike the puppy, however, you're the one who's tethered yourself to this leash. Only you can make the decision to set yourself free from it. Only you can break what holds you back from venturing out, exploring your world, and doing the things God has planned for you!

What would release you from the leash holding you back? Take a good snip at it today, even if it's a little one. Ask God to strengthen your resolve and your commitment to change. Hear Him say, "Go ahead and soar!"

**Bad habits are easier
to abandon today than tomorrow.**
Proverb

THE RIGHT WAY

Standing up for what's right isn't always easy or particularly comfortable. Sometimes it means taking an unpopular position among our friends, or insisting on fairness and justice for everyone involved, or opting to think for ourselves rather than rely on others to do our thinking for us.

Right now, there's probably something that everyone claims is "the truth" or has "really happened." It's all over social media, shared and re-shared until there's no one you know who hasn't heard it and accepted it as true. But is it true? Is the whole story out there, or only part of it? Are there other explanations or as yet unheard points of view? Are more flaws than facts making the rounds? It's worth thinking about, and asking others to think about, too.

Of course, you might not receive a round of applause for questioning current opinion. You might hear some criticism, maybe even get made fun of or ridiculed. Yet when you speak up, you influence others. Your courage nudges your friends to examine their own minds and see for themselves whether they have ever seriously questioned the validity of popular theories and constantly repeated claims.

You never know who you might inspire to speak up. Because of you, someone might be motivated to ask more questions and demand better answers. You change things for the better when you choose the right way, the truth. Your actions prove that although it's not easy, it can be done!

Care for the truth
more than what people think.
Aristotle

A GRANDLY HUMBLE PURPOSE

Some people spend a lifetime trying to figure out their life's grand purpose, but they never find it. Never, because they're looking for something grand! After all, they say to themselves, they haven't made earth-shattering discoveries in medicine or science; they haven't fed millions, founded hospitals, and brought about world peace. When they look at their life, all they see is one little person among many in a world of big needs and huge challenges.

It's when we look for our life's humble purpose that we discover its grand purpose. Our willingness to meet the simple, everyday needs of those around us opens us to the realization that we're here for a reason, and this is it. Our life takes on meaning in quiet and consistent service to even one child in need of encouragement, one person in need of compassion, one heart in need of generous, selfless love.

Look not to the future, but right now at the simple, everyday needs of those around you. See where you can help, serve, and contribute. Find your purpose in ordinary things, places where you can give something truly extraordinary—yourself.

Whether or not you ever get worldwide recognition for what you do, you're living a life of meaning and purpose whenever you take time to care. It's the reason our extraordinary God put you here. It's all part of His extraordinary, divine plan for your life.

**Pursue some path,
however narrow and crooked,
in which you can walk
with love and reverence.**
Henry David Thoreau

THE BIG PICTURE

Reality isn't always a pretty picture. The world is filled with hurt and brokenness, and our own lives have been touched and affected by our past and sometimes ongoing struggles.

Though we can't wish away uncomfortable, even ugly, facts about the world or alter our personal past, we can put them in perspective. How? Think of it this way:

You walk into a room where a big picture hangs on one wall. Immediately you run over to it and put your face right up to one section—a dismal, shadowy section. Would it be fair to say that the whole picture looks like that? Of course not!

But if you step back, you can see the whole picture. Right next to that ugly dot are bright colors, joyful swoops, whimsical squiggles, and serene pools of tranquil hues. Mysterious, hard-to-decipher contours adjoin clearly defined designs, and scratchy, rough surfaces give way to swaths of smooth, satiny textures. That's the wonderful world you live in! You may even recognize it as your own life.

See the whole picture. You will discover that many things make sense when you look at them in context. Sometimes you'll watch ugly splotches give way to beautiful shapes. You might realize how a later layer of paint clarified what had appeared to be a meaningless outline. As for an explanation for everything? You'll have to wait to ask the Master Artist!

Turn your stumbling blocks into stepping stones.

WHAT'S THE MATTER?

No doubt you care about the feelings of people you're close to. If someone is sad, worried, or hurting, you want to know why. "Tell me what happened!" you might say. If a friend is having a tough time right now, you hope the person will trust you enough to open up and let you know what's going on.

Even more, God wants you to tell Him how you feel and what you think. Of course He already knows everything about you—after all, He's God! But your act of expressing your worries, fears, and anxieties focuses your heart and mind on Him. When you come to Him in prayer, you show you believe in Him and trust in Him enough to share your inmost thoughts. God chooses to ask, "What's the matter?" and He chooses to listen. Your compassionate God invites you to open up and tell Him what's really bothering you.

You can pray anywhere, you know. You can pray sitting by yourself in your room or walking on your way to class in the morning. You can pray a prayer you read in a book or one that just pops into your mind. It can be long or short, spoken out loud or expressed in the depths of your heart.

"What's the matter?" you might ask someone you care about. "You can tell me!" And that's exactly what God says to you whenever you have something on your mind. Big problem? Little problem? Or just want to talk about it? It doesn't matter. If it concerns you, it concerns Him. He's listening, and He cares.

God loves to get knee-mail.

NOT MY MONKEY

No muss, no fuss—don't you wish life would go that smoothly? Well, it probably would without you-know-who and you-know-what always getting in your way! But given that some people and some things aren't going to change anytime soon (or ever), here are a few ideas you can think about that might help you cope.

First, concern for people and caring about the world is one thing, but worry is a big waste of time. If you can do something productive to show you care, then do it; but if not, your worrying isn't going to change a thing. Worry is an energy-draining, emotion-sapping habit that will make your life miserable. So why even start?

Second, you've heard the saying, "Not my monkey, not my circus." Watch out for people who try to get you involved in their problems or blame you for things that have nothing to do with you. You're accountable for yourself and what concerns you, and that's enough "monkeys" for any one person!

Third, learn to laugh. If you let little things throw you into a tizzy, you'll never get a moment's rest. Let trivial offenses and minor inconveniences slide by you like water off a duck's back. Forgive, laugh, and be kind, and you will be able to live at peace with yourself and the world.

Life isn't always simple and the way isn't always smooth, but it's how you take it that counts!

Every survival kit should include a sense of humor.

CALLING ALL RECYCLERS

Some people are good recyclers. From old socks, they'll make a ragdoll for a little niece or nephew. From a couple dozen colored bottles they find at a flea market, they'll create a piece of funky garden art.

Good recyclers are the ones who have a knack for finding value in what other people throw away. They have an eye for seeing what's usable and what's not...for separating treasures from trash.

Know what? You can do the same thing with everything that has happened to you! Rather than bemoan all the not-so-good times, decide you'll pick out all the great times to store in your memory bank. Why focus on a pile of old stuff that makes you sad? Highlight the best and let your memories make you smile!

If you want to keep smiling, do the same thing at the end of every day. Maybe it hasn't been a red-letter day and maybe nothing momentous has happened, but collect a few things that you liked from everything else—say a good laugh with a friend...that song you listened to...the steaming hot cup of chai tea you savored. Those are your daily treasures!

Reuse...recycle...reclaim your life with good thoughts, happy moments, and a heartfelt "thank you" to God, the source of all the good stuff!

**The key to happiness
is appreciating what you have.**

Couldn't Care More

You can tell when someone's really listening to you. Their eyes are focused on your face, not on who else might be coming into the room. There's no electronic device propped between your mouth and their ears. You don't have the feeling that they're going to change the subject to themselves as soon as they can get a word in edgewise. They are really listening!

If you're thinking, "I sure wish I had someone like that in my life," you can start the ball rolling right now. You can be someone like that. You can't force people to listen to you, but you can set the example by listening to them...really listening. All it takes is a little time to hear their words, understand their feelings, and care.

When you truly care about someone, you want to listen to him or her. You already know how your day went, but you won't know about her day until she tells you…and you're not likely to learn much unless you listen…and care about what she says. You're well acquainted with your own feelings on a particular topic, but you'll never figure out his opinion until he believes you'll take the time to hear him out…and care about what he says.

And if you need someone to listen to you right now, remember that God listens…and cares…like no one else. Talk to Him. He's all ears when it comes to the sound of your voice.

**When we listen with the heart,
we hear what is being said
with and without words.**
N. L. Roloff

TALL BRICK WALL

"I can't!" is like a big, heavy brick. The more
you say those words, the higher you stack the
bricks. Before long, you're standing in front of
a wall 90 feet tall and three feet thick. Well,
at least "I can't" has some truth to it now,
because no, you can't jump over it!

Maybe you could chisel away at it brick by
brick, but if you want to tear it down a little
faster, start at the foundation. Look for one
whopper of a rock labeled FEAR. Fear of
going through that interview process. Fear of
taking that competitive exam. Fear of meeting
new people. Fear of trying to make it on your
own in a new city. Fear of actually trying to
make a big dream come true.

It's always easier to say "I can't!" But every
time you say it, you give FEAR a brick to build
the wall you're faced with today. Fire FEAR as

your life coach, and try a few of those things you've always thought you couldn't do. You don't have to take a daring leap out of an airplane if you're afraid of heights, or address an auditorium full of people if public speaking leaves you a quivering mass of jelly. Start small, but start and keep going.

Watch the wall get shorter and shorter. Pretty soon you'll be able to jump over it. Then step over it. And then wonder if it was ever there in the first place.

**You gain strength,
courage and confidence by every
experience in which you really stop and
look fear in the face...
You must do what you think you cannot do.**
Eleanor Roosevelt

READY FOR ACTION

You've heard it said many times: "Reach for the stars!" "Pursue your goals!" "Go for it!" Those are fightin' words designed to get you pumped about getting out there and making things happen. But their effect fizzles fast without one crucial element—action. You have to make a move.

Sure, it's fun to talk about what you'd like to do, and you definitely should. As you toss around different ideas with friends and family, you might realize that you're more interested in one thing over another, and you keep going back to it. A particular direction, the longer you delve into it, becomes more appealing than others you've come up with. You can picture yourself there.

Also, people who know you best might have some pointers or suggestions to help you weigh your various options. You never know who might be able to put you in touch with someone who's already where you'd like to go.

No matter what you decide on or which direction you choose, you're bound to come up against unexpected challenges, a few setbacks and stumbles, and day-to-day hard work. Don't be afraid to ask for help and to follow the advice of experienced people who have your best interests at heart. Keep moving! And while you're busy reaching up, reach down to help someone who's just starting out. Someone who wants to do what you've done, be where you are.

Set your goals high. But remember that the first two letters of "goals" spell GO!

Shoot for the moon.
Even if you miss it,
you'll land among the stars.

Guaranteed Wealth

Are you rich or poor? Don't bother to check your bank balance or add your bills. Instead, see what's inside you. Are there assets, like faith, family, friends? Do you look at life on the bright side, and do you make it a point to be kind, gentle, loving, and forgiving? Are you generous with help, acknowledgement and encouragement? If you possess this kind of wealth, you are rich beyond measure!

In every life, however, there are liabilities. What are they? Things like giving in to popular prejudices...failing to stand up for what's right...joining mean-spirited discussions and uncivil debates...contributing to someone's struggles...refusing to apologize, forgive, make amends where needed. Do you recognize a few of these liabilities as your own? Just like a high credit card balance, they need to go away.

God's Spirit, who works in your heart, can help you do it. Tell Him about the particular liabilities that bother you, and ask for His help. Let Him enable you to start building assets instead of gathering liabilities when you find yourself with that hurtful remark on the tip of your tongue...does it really need to be said? That carelessly spoken insult you heard...do you really have to make a big deal out of it?

Happiness, strength, and peace of mind... those are the assets God has for you. And the best thing is, He wants to make you very rich indeed, if you will just let Him.

**Be awake in every moment
to feel each joy life is giving you.**
N. L. Roloff

TIME MANAGEMENT

"When all is said and done"—well, don't ever expect to get it all said and done! If there aren't job responsibilities, appointments, meeting times, workshops scheduled, then there are friends to visit, interests to pursue, and things you've always wanted to do. If you're like many people, you're so busy that you have trouble finding time to eat and sleep!

Yes, there are many things you *must* do and many things you *want* to do. A busy schedule of productive activities gives meaning and direction to life, and that's truly important. But it's possible to get so busy with important things that you leave no time for what's most important, and that's time to think about more than simply what's going on outside of you. Time to appreciate what's going on *inside* of you. Time with God.

Even a few minutes each day to reflect on words from Scripture or a short devotional reading helps you get in touch with your innermost needs. Prayer—whether you pray while walking, running, biking, working out, riding the bus or sitting quietly in your room—connects you to the source of life and breath, wisdom and peace. Regular and attentive meditation on God's love for you builds lasting self-esteem, deep gratitude, and the will and ability to love others as yourself.

Whatever your calendar looks like, practice good time management by putting in time for God. After all, the giver of time deserves a little of it, doesn't He? There is nothing you can say or do that's more important.

**Time is a very precious gift of God;
so precious that it's only given
to us moment by moment.**
Amelia Barr

NEED TITLE

What's the difference between honest marketing and deceptive advertising? It's not a question that concerns service and product providers only. It's a question that has to do with each one of us when it comes to telling our story.

Your story, just like everyone else's story, includes at least a few less-than-stellar chapters. No one is immune from taking a wrong turn from time to time...from making a bad decision when young, but whose consequences limit options and opportunities years into the future...from making a mistake that you have to explain somehow and in some way to those who need to know. An interviewer asks. A close friend inquires. A potential partner wonders. Do you want them to get their answers from someone else, or from you?

But rather than letting dark details back you into deceptive advertising, treat them the way someone who passed Honest and Open Marketing 101 with flying colors would.

In situations where you must deal with an unpleasant detail, name it. Don't try to cover it up or give it a euphemism that could signal an inability to face facts. But follow up by saying what you learned from the experience...how you have used what happened to you to help others avoid the same mistake...what you've done in the meantime to show you're wiser and more mature today than yesterday.

Tell your story, emphasizing the best, in keeping with the truth. It makes good sense... it's the right thing.

**Wisdom comes from experience,
and experience comes from making
mistakes and learning from them.**
N. L. Roloff

ONLY YOU

Imagine yourself walking along a rural road. You come to a big, wide-branched fruit tree standing in the middle of an open field. You're intrigued and you wouldn't mind a bit of shade right now, so you go over to it and sit down under it. Only then do you realize that the tree's branches are heavy with fruit of all kinds—peaches, apples, apricots, pears, plums, pomegranates, cherries, and oranges!

Unbelievable? It sure is. Apple trees bear apples, and they don't apologize for not producing a bumper crop of peaches. Cherry trees bear cherries, and they aren't intimidated into thinking that they really ought to put out a few plums just to show they can do it. Orange trees bear oranges, and it makes little sense to berate an orange grove for its lack of pears.

Those trees aren't dumb. They bear one kind of fruit, the one kind that God intended them to bear, and they do it well.

How about you? What do you do especially well? God gave each person unique and special abilities and talents, and He didn't make an exception with you! To find your purpose... to discover meaning...to know the reality of peace and fulfillment, appreciate the way He created you and the unique gifts you have to offer.

**God made you for a very
special purpose...
in this time,
at this place,
for His plan.**

ALL THE BEST

You've seen the words on greeting cards and you've heard them from family members and friends—"Best wishes!" "Success to you!" "Sky's the limit!"

Yet sometimes these well-intentioned phrases don't reflect your reality. You wish you could feel wildly successful, but right now, it's more fantasy than fact.

If your reality isn't greeting-card perfect at the moment, stop what you're doing and take a moment to focus on God. Think about His awesome love for you and power to make things happen. Take each worry and concern and disappointment and turn them into a prayer. Just praying about whatever is making you anxious will help restore your enthusiasm and renew your happiness. That's because prayer reminds you that you're not alone. God is always with you and at work behind the scenes.

Remember that He has a special place for you, a place where you will be able to use those many gifts He has given to you. A place where you can learn and grow, create and contribute, meet new people and make a real difference in the world.

That's truly "all the best," isn't it? That's success, and the sky's the limit!

**I have not failed.
I've just found 10,000 ways
that won't work.**
Thomas A. Edison

It's Mind-Boggling!

When you were growing up, the whole world
was new to you. By exploring your neigh-
borhood, going to the park, and taking field
trips, no doubt something as simple as a bee
drawing nectar from a flower held you in
rapt attention...the feel of a calf's soft coat
made you squeal with pleasure...the salty
air at the seashore put you in immediate
sandcastle-building mode.

Now that you've seen more of the world,
don't forget its wonder. Let the creativity,
diversity, and intricacy of every God-ordained
detail of this universe boggle your mind. Don't
take for granted what has become familiar—
trees, flowers, and sunsets. Animals and
insects, sparkling stars and shiny moon.

Even though you're going in a new direction
now, take your sense of awe with you. Not
only does wonder add joy to your life, it also

reminds you that there's something bigger and more powerful than yourself out there—the creator of this wonder-full world!

Continue to see, notice, ponder, question, and read. Allow yourself to be boggled by the mysteries of life. Consider the significance of every God-created thing, from the biggest to the smallest. Be in awe of God and the work of His hands every day!

**God took the time to create
this awesome world...
Never be too busy to appreciate it.**

Useless Baggage

Lots of people lug the past around with them. They shoulder regrets and grudges, pick at old wounds, and won't let go of hurts and disappointments they experienced years and years ago. It's as if they've packed a big trunk full of outdated, ill-fitting clothes and insist upon dragging it everywhere!

The past is about more than what has happened in your life so far. It's also about what you lacked, what you wish you had been able to do, what actually happened, and the events you'd give anything to change. But God doesn't rewrite history. What He does, however, is help you put it in perspective and take from yesterday only what you need to make today and tomorrow better.

There's nothing you've done that God cannot forgive. When you allow Him into your life,

you can experience the freedom of forgiveness, whether it's yourself or someone else
that you're struggling to forgive. If you keep
reliving an unfortunate event or can't seem
to get away from distressing memories, ask
God to put someone in your life who can help
you. And then accept their help. Get rid of
the baggage you don't need to carry around
anymore.

**Unload that useless baggage...
you'll have more room
to carry self-confidence.**

Some Things

When you wake up in the morning, hunger is your body's way of saying, "I want food!" If you feed it a bowl of cereal or a couple of scrambled eggs, it'll be happy—for a couple hours anyway!

When your body tells you what it needs, it's best to listen. But your mind is not quite as straight-forward as your stomach. It often confuses need-to-have with wants-to-have. It's swayed by things like emotion and advertising, personal habit and other people's possessions. Sometimes what you see, hear, and feel seems like just the thing that will make you happy, but when you get it you realize it's just another thing that hasn't lived up to its promise.

Contentment is the source of true and lasting happiness. Without it, that longing for the next big "thing" will leave you constantly feeling hungry and dissatisfied with your life.

But know this— contentment is not resignation! It's not about slacking off and never striving to make life better or achieve worthwhile goals. Rather, contentment is being thankful for what you have instead of hankering after what you don't. The more thankful you are, the more contented you'll become—and the happier you'll feel about yourself and the world around you. Because, as you probably already know, life is more than "things."

**It is not how much we have,
but how much we enjoy,
that makes happiness.**
Charles Spurgeon

HAVE FUN!

Whoever says Christians can't or shouldn't have fun doesn't know much about Christ! Jesus, although the Savior of the world, took time out to play. He attended weddings, joined in celebrations, hung out with friends, and went to dinners and feasts. He was known to take naps during storms and go on long walks in the hills when He needed a timeout.

While accomplishing His ministry of teaching and preaching, Jesus spent time with kids. When His grown-up followers tried to shoo the kids away, Jesus invited them to come to Him, and not to instruct them in religion. He enjoyed their giggles, their antics, their playfulness to the fullest—and it's not hard to imagine Him throwing His head back in laughter at one of their silly jokes!

If years of schoolwork, extra-curricular activities, and community service have pushed fun into the background, it's time to bring it up front. Follow Jesus, who knew how to laugh, play, rest, and reflect. There's plenty of serious, significant stuff you still need to think about and do. But each new day also extends an invitation to fun, joy, discovery, laughter, and play. Show 'em how Christians have fun!

It is a happy talent to know how to play.
Ralph Waldo Emerson

ALL GOOD GIFTS

It's great fun to get a gift, especially when it's for no other reason than because someone likes you and wants to give it to you. But do you know that you began receiving gifts from God even before you were born?

These gifts came all wrapped up in your own tiny body. Some came fully assembled, like the gift of perfect pitch, an analytical mind, a creative streak, or a quirky sense of humor. Other gifts might come to you as do-it-yourself kits. You have the opportunity to put these gifts together as you learn, mature, and experience life. These include talents like the ability to draw a portrait, learn a skill, or master a foreign language. The variety of gifts God gives is as diverse as the people who receive them.

Do you know what your God-given gifts are? Consider what you really like to do. Think about areas in which you excel. Be completely honest, even if it feels a bit like bragging. If you're still not sure what gifts you possess, ask those closest to you what they see. You might be surprised at how many gifts you have! And then put each one to use. Sharing your gifts with others is like sending a heartfelt Thank-You note to God.

Every good gift and
every perfect gift is from above...
James 1:17

DRESS FOR SUCCESS

It's been said that "clothes make the man."
Or woman! But while what you choose to
wear projects something about you—your
tastes and values, how you want to be
perceived by others, what you believe is
suitable for the occasion—your clothes are
nothing more than window dressing. Clothes
can never "make" the man or woman because
they don't have that kind of power.

It's the attitude you put on that really counts,
and it's how you treat others that makes you
who you are and determines how people see
you. You can be dressed to the nines, but with
a sour or defensive look on your face, you
will never look your best. You might walk into
an interviewer's office perfectly outfitted,
but rudeness, arrogance, or bad manners
will completely undo your initially favorable
appearance.

So go ahead and dress for success. Pay attention to what you put on, because it's the first thing people see when they meet you. But make certain that your clothing includes things like kindness, thoughtfulness, generosity, and respect for others. They're always flattering, always appropriate, always fit just right, and never go out of style.

Clothe yourself with compassion, kindness, humility, gentleness and patience.
Colossians 3:12 NIV

FILL 'ER UP!

Is the glass half full or half empty? Or does the whole question leave you glassy eyed? Well, it all depends on how you look at it!

The person who finds something wrong with everything is just as misguided as the one who believes no flaws exist anywhere. As it is, our world is full of positive, exciting, and uplifting concepts, words, and actions; and at the same time, sad facts and painful events. The glass is both half full and half empty. That's why a balanced approach is realistic, as well as productive because it celebrates what's right and seeks solutions for what could be better.

When God looks at you, He sees your many strengths. After all, He gave them to you! He also recognizes your weaknesses. But instead of simply leaving them there, He invites you to bring them to Him. A desire to do better?

There's a half-full glass He can fill. Only a few drops of peace and joy in your life? Let Him take it from there, because He knows how to make your heart and soul brim over with blessings.

Look at where you are now. Give thanks, and let God fill you up with His love.

Most people are about as happy as they make up their minds to be.
Abraham Lincoln

FOR FREE

From getting an education to buying a cup of coffee, everything seems expensive these days! Thank goodness, though, that the most satisfying things in life are free.

Take friendship. Friends care, listen, and understand, with no meter attached. There's no charge for being a friend, or for putting yourself out there and making friends. No price tag on the privilege of mulling over a clever saying, reflecting on a meaningful quote, or doodling around with a new idea in your head.

There's no charge for dreaming. No matter how high your hopes, how big your imagination, how lofty your aspirations, the cost is zilch. And who knows where your dreams will take you, once you start acting on them?

Spend a few minutes counting the blessings
that come free from the hand of God. Then
remember that it doesn't cost anything,
either, to do a lot of good in the world. Your
welcoming smile, friendly word, casual "hi,"
and simple kindnesses go a long way in letting
others know they're noticed and appreciated.
Those little freebies you spread around make
the day brighter for others, and you'll find that
they brighten your day, too. For free.

**Kindness costs nothing—
but it's the most precious gift
you can give someone.**

LOOK AT YOU NOW!

Say you've got a project you want to take on. Fired up, you tell someone about it. There's a deafening pause, and then they give you The Look—that one that says, loud and clear, "I don't want to burst your bubble, but...." What happens? The Look is as sharp as a pin pressed into a balloon and has the same effect. Pffft! As the balloon goes, so goes your bubble. And your enthusiasm.

So what to do? Sure, you can mumble something about how silly you are to even think of such a thing, and drop the whole idea. Or you can burst their bubble by taking The Look as a challenge. Don't bother telling them that you're going through with it, though, because they'll only nod and smile. Instead, delve into your project and give it your best effort. Consistent and persistent work will get you where you want to go. And when you get there, The Lookers can only stand back and look at you now! Need you say more?

Here's another thing—talk to people who believe in you, who support you, who will boost you up instead of putting you down. You're too busy for any other kind of conversation.

Keep way from people who try to belittle your ambitions. Small people always do that, but the really great make you feel that you, too, can become great.
Mark Twain

No, Nope, Nada

God answers prayer, and sometimes His answer is a resounding "No"! While it's not the answer you want to hear at the time, you'll often realize later that it was the right answer. You might even say a prayer of gratitude for His well-placed "No"! Time has shown you that what you had prayed for was not important, not necessary, or just plain dumb. (Remember those earnest yearnings of your younger self? Aren't you glad God didn't give you everything you wanted so desperately?)

Thank God—really thank Him!—that He's not an indulgent uncle who sits on a cloud and grants your every wish. Instead, He's your creator, who knows you better than you know yourself. He's your protector, who refuses to give you something that will hurt or harm you. He's your counselor, who will never mince words with you. When He says "No", there's a real-life reason. He's your guide, who will always lead you in the right direction. Though the way may be unclear to you, it's crystal-clear to Him.

God sees yesterday, today, and forever. He's God. That's why when He speaks, you can be sure He knows what He's talking about.

**A bend in the road is not
the end of the road—
unless you fail to make the turn.**

GOD'S FACE

Next time you're sitting in a coffee shop, out shopping, or walking along a busy sidewalk, notice how many people look happy. Probably very few. You're more likely to find more pinched faces, furrowed brows, and fixed frowns than you can count!

Unfortunately, those of us who know God loves us are often the worst offenders. Though God provides us with His presence, we still look at the world through fear-tinted glasses. Though He blesses us with peace of mind as we put our trust in Him, we walk around as if everyone else is out to get us. Though God has filled our hearts with His joy, we often forget to tell our face about it.

Many people you see each day are dealing with overwhelming stress, huge personal problems, and fears beyond your comprehension. And they do not know God. They have no idea that someone-out-there loves them and cares about them. Sometimes all it takes to give them a glimpse of their loving God is a warm smile on the lips of a passerby and a set of friendly eyes seeing them as a real person instead of a face in the crowd. Could you be the one God is asking to be His face today?

A smile is a light in the window of a face that shows someone is home.

Wit and Wisdom

Someone says something, and a clever zinger zaps right to the tip of the tongue. But most of us have learned through trial and error (lots and lots of error!) that it's wise to firmly zip the lips.

Zingers that go no further than the back of your teeth save you embarrassment and avoid insulting others. Even if you know that your friends would find the remark terribly funny, your willingness to "say anything" would leave them wary of you. Who knows who might be the next victim of your piercing wit? When your silence replaces a funny but unkind comment, however, you come across as someone who's mature, caring, and in control. That's as important among your friends as it is in a business meeting; with your family as it is with the special person you love; in personal conversations as it is online.

Yes, it takes effort and forethought to say something witty, yet wise; clever, yet kind-hearted; astute, yet attractive. Mainly, though, it takes a heart filled with empathy for others and a mind determined not to nurture unkind judgments about anyone. If it's not in your thoughts, you don't have to worry about it coming out of your mouth!

What is held in our heart is heard in our speech.

Action-Packed Hunch

Intuition—your gut feelings—and action work together. For example, suppose your intuition tells you something's not quite right about what someone's telling you. Or the great offer is just a little too good to be true. So let that be your kick-in-the-pants call to action! Dig a little deeper into the matter. Ask questions, find out more, learn why you're being told one thing but not another. What you discover could be significant.

Your God-given voice of intuition, based in the knowledge of His love for you and compassion for all, is meant to inspire a God-given plan of action. While you might be eager to dive right into a project, intuition urges you to hold off until you're sure about what you're getting into. Acting on intuition might pull you in another direction...take up time you didn't plan on...get in the way of what you really want to do. But not acting on intuition silences the voice, the guidance, the wisdom of God in your heart.

As you meet new people, deal with new situations, and grapple with new decisions, honor your intuition. Listen to it, because intuition needs to walk hand-in-hand with action. They're best buds.

Dear God,
Through my experiences today,
please grant me insight and wisdom.

AMBITION CALLING

"What's your ambition?" You've probably heard that question many times lately! So you've told your well-wishers that you want to pursue an advanced degree...join a corporation...start your own business...earn a certificate in your chosen field...explore the world for a year or so. Because you have ambition, you have a good reason to get up in the morning and look forward to a new day.

But ambition is like a two-edged sword. Though it slices through lethargy and laziness and gets us doing something productive, it can also take over our lives. Out-of-control ambition focuses our attention solely on ourselves and what we want, so we cut down everyone in our path as we clamber for the corner office, the next big scoop, the highest salary, the most authority, the top position.

Like so many of God's good gifts, your ambition can work for bad or good. It can cut down the people around you, or it can lead you on a wonderful adventure as you learn from the people ahead of you, lean on those beside you, and teach those following you. Ambition can rule your life, or it can infuse your life with direction, meaning, and purpose. It all depends on how you wield the sword.

English is a funny language.
A fat chance and a slim chance
mean the same thing.

PERFECT LOVE

Most people hope to find true love. Maybe you already know who it is you want to spend the rest of your life with. Or perhaps you're still looking for that one person who will love you always.

The good news is that you don't have to look for a love like that, because it's already yours. God has loved you since before you even knew He existed! And He'll continue loving you beyond the end of time. With God, there's no "till death do us part." His love is not only true, it's truly timeless.

It's also unconditional. That means you can't do anything to lose His love because you didn't do anything to gain it—God is love, and He loves you. Period. Honestly, isn't that the best love story ever?

There will be others who will love you in this life. Friends and family. Perhaps a spouse one day, and children. Their love will change your life in many wonderful ways. But there will inevitably be tough times, as well. Every human relationship faces them. That's because people are fallible. They make mistakes. At times, they do and say selfish things.

Others – even those who love you very deeply – may let you down at times. God won't, He can't. God is perfect and so is His love. So don't be afraid to give your heart fully to God. You can be sure He'll treat you right.

**I have loved thee
with an everlasting love...**
Jeremiah 31:3

By Faith

You can board a plane and fly around the world without understanding anything about aerodynamics. You can push "Send" on an email without being able to explain how it arrives on your friend's computer screen. You can swallow an aspirin without knowing precisely how it relieves a headache.

There are lots of things you do every day "by faith". You trust that the pilot knows how to operate the plane, the computer programmer has gotten it right, and the pharmacist has created an effective remedy. You rely on these people, even if you never see them face to face.

That's how it is with God. You can't look Him in the eye, but you can rely on the work of His hands. You can see the intricacy of creation. You can remember how He has answered your prayers in the past. You can read in the Bible how He has helped others throughout history. You can hear Him whisper through the voice of your conscience.

You don't have to fully understand God to trust Him and follow Him, in the same way you don't have to fully understand chemistry to take an aspirin and appreciate what it can do for you. The more you invite God to be involved in every area of your life, the more you'll learn to trust Him. And the stronger your faith will grow.

**Faith is daring the soul
to go where the eyes can't see.**

You're a Trailblazer!

A jet crossing the sky or a snail inching along the ground share something in common. They both leave a trail. There's evidence of their existence even after they've moved far out of sight. Graduate, the same is true of you.

Your "trail" is etched on the hearts of those who have loved, taught, guided, supported, and encouraged you all these years. They know you and care about you, and celebrate your talents and accomplishments, your achievements and goals. But unlike the trail of a jet or snail, yours won't be erased by wind or rain. You're a permanent part of history—and history has been changed by your presence.

No matter what you do or where you go, you will leave a trail behind in the thoughts, memories, and experiences of people you meet.

What you say and do affects how others see you, and sometimes even affects the way they see themselves. Your trail can either show others what not to do, or provide a shining example of what it means to live with faith, purpose, and everyday kindness.

Let your words and actions become a path others would be blessed to follow.

Blessed is the influence of one true, loving human soul on another.
George Eliot

Open To Love

We were created not only to give love, but to receive it. Sounds simple enough, doesn't it? Yet for many of us, receiving love doesn't come easy.

For example, suppose someone offers you a birthday present – a really BIG gift. The box is so huge, you have to open your arms extra wide before you can take hold of it. What happens when you do that? You become vulnerable. Your defenses fall. And then to fully take hold of the gift, you have to pull it in close to you so you don't drop or damage it.

That's the way it is when receiving the gift of love. You can't accept it if you've got the "arms" of your heart crossed in front of you. You can't take hold of it if you keep your hands clasped tightly to your side. Rather, you need to allow yourself to become vulnerable.

The more you accept someone's love, the more you will trust that person, the safer you will feel and the more open you can be. When you're open, you're more honest, real, and sincere.

Open yourself up to receive the love that God and those around you are holding out to you. Appreciate it. Delight in it. Give thanks for it. And definitely feel free to return it!

To love at all is to be vulnerable.
C. S. Lewis

HOLD ON TO HOPE

You probably already know this—the odds of winning the lottery are not in your favor. You're more likely to write the next block-buster thriller, become president of the United States, or be crushed to death by a vending machine, than win! Yet more than half the population of the US plays at least once a year. Why? Hope. Players hold onto the hope that the lottery will be their ticket to financial security.

It's important to hold onto hope. Without it, it's easy to lose heart. But it's also important to base your hope on something real, something lasting. Resting your hope simply on positive thinking or fervent wishing is as effective as rubbing a lucky rabbit's foot.

God is the only rock-solid source of real hope in this life. He loves you and wants what's best for you. He knows your heart and hears your prayers—and promises to answer them. That doesn't mean you're a shoe-in to win the lottery if you pray. In addition to "Yes," He also answers "No" and "Not now."

Do all you can to help what you hope for become reality. Then trust God with the rest. Whatever God's answer, you can rest in the hope that He'll see you through.

With God all things are possible.
Mark 10:27

IQ vs. WQ (WISDOM QUOTIENT)

You've graduated—you're smart! Being smart has its advantages. Smarts can help you get on a game show or go for a higher degree. It can let you hold your own in intelligent conversations and allows you to solve complex problems. Smarts can earn the respect of those around you, too. But without wisdom, all the intelligence in the world is little more than the human version of a computer hard drive.

While intelligence is often measured by an IQ test, wisdom is measured by the quality of your life and relationships. How much you know isn't important unless you also know how to apply it in a way that honors God and respects others. For instance, smart people may know how to cheat on their income taxes. Wise people, however, understand that this isn't a smart thing to do. Smart people may be able to name every book in the Bible. Wise people know how to relate biblical teachings to real life.

You're already smart. Now ask God to supply the wisdom you need when you're unsure what to do. With His help, you can make wiser decisions than you ever could on your own, no matter how high your IQ score!

The highest form of wisdom is kindness.
Talmud

In Tune With Your Purpose

If you want to compose music for a band or orchestra, you have to understand what each instrument can and cannot do. One instrument might be just the right thing for a solo, for example, while others produce the perfect backup sound. Unless each instrument plays its part, however, even the world's greatest composition is nothing more than notes on a page.

God is the composer of the symphony of life. Each person is like a unique instrument with a specific part to play. In the same way that a violin can't fill in for the kettledrum, you cannot fill the purpose of your next door neighbor. Or vice versa.

Each individual has a singular blend of skills, knowledge, experience and personality— as well as a specific time and place in history.

When people use all of these in harmony with what God has planned, something beautiful happens. They not only accomplish amazing things, they experience a true sense of purpose in their lives.

If you're unclear about the part you were created to play, ask those who know you well what you excel at and where they think your gifts could make the most positive impact. Pray. Then, play. Try something new. The parts you play will vary during different seasons of your life. But practice—mixed with love— makes perfect.

Great minds have purposes, others have wishes.
Washington Irving

Declaration Of Dependence

It's true. God has lots of wonderful things in mind for you. However, living life as a lone ranger isn't one of them. His design for us is to live in community with each other and with Him. In the famous words of John Donne, "No man is an island." No woman, either. We're all interconnected! Our lives not only brush up against each other, we get the most out of life when we work together, form relationships, and depend on one another for encouragement and support.

Yet some people see dependence as a sign of weakness. They refuse to ask for help when they need it. Sure, they're willing to lend a hand to others, but when it comes to their own needs, they're determined to go it alone. But what they want you to see as strength is often rooted in ego, fear, and pride. True strength is evident when we invite others into our lives, especially into those broken places—where we have to admit that we're far from self-sufficient.

Help is close at hand. Friends, family, neighbors, the church community, doctors, counselors, mentors, your heavenly Father...the list of those ready to come to your aid is long. All you need to do is ask.

Weak things united become strong.
Thomas Fuller

Jump For Joy

Wouldn't it be wonderful if happiness is what God has in mind for you? It just may be. But constant happiness isn't something God has promised to provide. He has promised something better, though; something richer, deeper, and longer lasting. He has promised joy.

Joy is better because it doesn't rely on the condition of your circumstances, as happiness does. Instead, it depends solely on the state of your mind, heart, and soul. The more you rest in the knowledge that God is in control—and you're not—the more joy you'll find flowing through your life.

Awe, anticipation, enthusiasm, gratitude, love, inner peace—that's joy. It may even feel like happiness, but less giddy and fickle. Joy is a sense of profound satisfaction that fills you when you see a spectacular sunset or the face of someone you love; when you achieve a long-desired goal or receive the best opportunity you ever could have imagined. In little ways throughout the day, joy reminds you that life is good, even when circumstances could be better.

Joy isn't something you need to pursue. It's already there, residing within you. The more you follow God's will for you, the more you'll be able to sift what's of value from what's not—and the more joy you'll experience in your life.

Joy is peace dancing.
Peace is joy at rest.
Frederick Brotherton Meyer

GROW ON!

You're a grownup now! No longer a pre-schooler, kindergartener, middle schooler, high schooler, because you've graduated! You've changed and grown and matured. Imagine, though, if at this stage in life you continued to act like a toddler—whining, pouting, insisting on having your own way. For sure, you would have very few friends!

Growth is part of God's design. People enter the world as babies and then grow to become adults. But physical growth is just one area in which we're meant to mature. We get the most out of life when we continue to grow in every area of our lives, including emotionally, mentally, socially, and spiritually.

So, how does who you are today compare with who you were last year? Have you grown in positive ways? If so, what has encouraged you to grow? If not, what do you think is holding you back? More than with physical growth, you have control over how well you grow mentally and spiritually. You can choose to put childish habits and attitudes aside. You can grow in your relationships with God and others by choosing to spend time, to listen, to learn, and to love. Don't settle for growing up without growing into the mature person you have the opportunity to become.

**Sometimes growing up means
leaving behind what has been,
and looking forward to what can be.**
N. L. Roloff

LIFE UNPLUGGED

Text, tweets, social media, conference calls, video chats...staying connected is easier than ever before. It's also more expected than ever before. If life takes you away from an Internet connection, you feel as though you need to apologize to those who aren't able to get ahold of you right... this... minute!

Unfortunately, staying constantly connected can keep you disconnected from what matters most. The relentless beeping, buzzing, and ringing makes every little thing you do an exercise in multitasking. That means it's hard to give your total attention to any one thing at a time.

Although technology enables you to keep up with your friends, and work better and more effectively, it doesn't mean that you can't benefit from powering down once in a while. Some vital parts of life thrive best in the quiet moments. In silence, you can hear God's still, small voice. Without interruptions, you can thoughtfully sort through problems and discover solutions. Minus distractions from the outside, you can sit down with another person and really listen to what they have to say.

Schedule quiet spots in your day. Turn off your cellphone and computer. Tuck the earbuds away. Sit and think. Or listen. Or pray. Or simply enjoy the sanctuary of silence.

**In quietness and in confidence
shall be your strength.**
Isaiah 30:15

THE CHOICE IS YOURS

Puppets are fun to play with. But no one wants to be one. Yet some people imagine God as a mighty Puppet Master in the sky. They believe God has a plan for their life and that's what's going to happen. Period.

Does God have plans for you? You bet. But that doesn't mean He's pulling the strings behind the scenes to make all of them happen exactly the way He'd like. Nor will he "manipulate" you to make you act exactly the way He'd like. No—He's given you free will. He has given you the power to say "yes" or "no." You can choose whether to walk toward Him or away from Him. Is it wise to follow where He leads? Absolutely. He loves you and wants the very best for your life. He can see farther ahead than you can, and He would love to steer you around bumps in the road that you are unable to see from where you stand now.

The choice, however, is up to you. Of course, free will doesn't always play out well. Some people choose to lead selfish lives, cause conflict, and hurt others. This is not God's plan for their lives—or those they hurt along the way. That's the cost of free will.

So why did He give you free will? Because He's not looking for a relationship with a puppet. You can only give and receive love when there are no strings attached. Love has to be a choice or it isn't love at all. Choose wisely.

A loving heart is the truest wisdom.
Charles Dickens

Team Humanity

When you picture a team, you're likely to think of a group of people getting together to play a sport, solve a problem, or handle a class project. But there's another kind of team, and that team includes you and all those around you—family members, friends, classmates, coworkers, and anyone else you meet during the day. You might call it "Team Humanity." And to be considered a Most Valuable Player, all you have to do is cheer for those around you!

An effective cheer can be as quick as a compliment or spontaneous high-five. It can mean a longer-term commitment, such as standing by a friend during a difficult time. You can cheer someone on by offering words of encouragement; you can provide moral support just by being there for them. Cheering is all about doing what it takes to build up those around you to help bring out the best in them.

You, too, need cheerleaders in your life.
That's why healthy relationships are so vital!
They make you stronger, more courageous,
more confident, and downright happier.

Consider who's on your team. How can you
cheer them on? What are they saying to cheer
you on? Take their words to heart. Believe
those who believe in you!

**...Encourage one another
and build each other up.**
1 Thessalonians 5:11 NIV

Take Hold Of Today

You've probably heard the phrase, "carpe diem." It's often translated as "seize the day," but a more accurate translation would be "pluck the day." It refers to the way you might pluck a piece of fruit off a tree—not too early when it's sour, or too late when it's rotten. You want to pluck fruit precisely when it's sweet, ripe, and ready to eat.

One of the most valuable gifts God extends to you is time. But the problem with time is that it refuses to stand still! You can't "save" time in a bottom drawer and then bring it out at a later date. You have to use it today, because right now—and right now only—the present moment is ripe and ready to savor.

This doesn't mean you should cram every waking moment with activity. That's more like frantically seizing than thoughtful plucking!

It could be that the best use of time is to watch the sun set, take a nap or just sit and hold someone's hand. The opportunity you have right now will never come around again in quite the same way.

The time you have right now is a priceless gift, yours to unwrap, to enjoy, to appreciate. Take hold of today.

Happiness, not in another place,
but this place...
not for another hour, but this hour.
Walt Whitman

Strategic Thinking

"Together we stand," the motto goes, "and divided we fall." That's why ancient clans banded together and why nations forge alliances with one another today. A nation with nothing to rely on but its own strength is easily overcome. As a member of a strong alliance, it presents a far more formidable adversary.

It's our spiritual alliances that can either help or hinder our ability to fend off temptation and stand up under pressure. Allied with the notion that we've got what it takes to live a life free of fault, we'll soon find ourselves blindsided by our own pride. If we look for security in money, health, fame, or power, these things will prove useless when it comes to the assaults of doubt, despair, or despondency. If we join with those who ignore God's guidelines for living, we'll fall right along with them and suffer the same sad consequences.

High-level strategic thinking goes into alliances between nations. Governments consider where they're vulnerable, and then decide from whom they can seek the strength and protection they desire. As an individual, your spiritual alliance with God is your lasting security, your undefeatable power, and where you can confidently put your trust. It's strategic thinking at its best.

I would rather walk with God in the dark than go alone in the light.
Mary Gardiner Brainard

ENTHUSIASTIC RESPONSE

Some things need to get done, whether we enjoy doing them or not. So we set about the hated assignment, project, or obligation feeling like a toddler who's sitting at the kitchen table under command to finish his peas and carrots. The vegetables aren't going to taste good to the child, no matter how flavorful they really are; and the time spent staring at the plate and pouting only puts off the unescapable—the vegetables must be eaten.

When enthusiasm doesn't happen naturally, why not make it happen? We can coax it into being by remembering *why* we're going about the task and then thanking God. A dentist appointment means we have access to health care—many people aren't so fortunate. A routine function is an important contribution to the success of the project—what a privilege to be part of it. Long evenings of study advance our knowledge and expertise—we'll appreciate our diligence in the future.

Gratitude brings enthusiasm, and enthusiasm lightens any task and brightens the time we spend doing it. Though we might have a tough time convincing a vegetable-phobic toddler of this truth, it's something we can understand. What's more, we can start putting it into practice immediately simply by choosing to be enthusiastic!

Nothing is so contagious as enthusiam.
Samuel Taylor Coleridge

Life Lived Forward

Few of us can look back on every year and season of life with complete satisfaction. Recalling what we said to a particular person or how we acted in a certain situation makes us cringe. We wince to remember instances where our immaturity was obvious to all, and the consequences of our actions foreseen by everyone except ourselves. Yes, there are plenty of moments in life we would just as soon forget!

Though complete dismissal of past failings may elude us, God has put them behind Him. Whatever has happened or how we've acted in our growing-up years is of no account to God, who desires to lead us forward. He doesn't care where we've been, but He cares passionately about where we're going.

There's no issue, problem, or mistaken belief that God will hold against you or refuse to forgive. Rather, He uses these things to draw

you closer to Him as you approach Him
with a humble, repentant heart. It's through
your slips and stumbles that He teaches you,
reminding you to lean on Him, listen to Him,
and love Him the way He loves you.

He renews the heart. He transforms the soul.
He brings you forward in newness of life.

**To dwell on the past
or worry about the future
only robs you of today.**

ALL FOR YOU

"It's all up to you!" You might have heard those words from someone urging you to make the most of your opportunities. That's because no matter how many things others do for you, they can't give you a positive attitude, instill genuine industriousness, and empower your creativity. Those things are up to you!

There's something, however, that is not up to you—and that's God's love. The moment you start placing conditions on His love for you, there's no relief from wondering whether you've made one too many mistakes. There's no rest from frantically doing as many good things as you can to earn His favor—but exactly how many gold stars does it take to make God smile?

Repeatedly, Scripture assures us that it isn't all up to us. In fact, God's love isn't even a little bit up to us, but entirely up to God. He chooses to love us. His love is complete, so there's no possibility of changing or modifying His love. It's simply there for us to delight in, rely on, and accept with open arms.

Faith in God's love removes the weight of anxiety, self-condemnation, and doubts about self-worth. The reality of His love is nothing less than His eternal promise: "I have done it all for you."

**Though our feelings come and go,
God's love for us does not.**
C. S. Lewis

SPIRITUAL LIFE

Graduation is one of life's milestones. As we pass these markers, we might pause to reflect on the significance of what has happened and what it means from here on. Very often, these thoughts take a spiritual turn.

At this point, perhaps you are wondering how you can live a meaningful, vital, and vigorous spiritual life, yet still pursue an advanced degree, find employment, or explore the world. Some people think the two are mutually exclusive! But that's far from the case. Spiritual people are everywhere—from corporations to kitchens, bustling cities to sleepy towns.

If you want to live a spiritual life, you need look no further than to the people right around you. Whether you see them in the classroom, corridors, airline terminals, or right in your own living room, they are people God loves. They hunger for love and care, help and encouragement, understanding and compassion. When you give of yourself to them, you grow in wisdom and understanding, in goodness and godliness. Serving others is the core, the essence, of spiritual living.

Truly spiritual people are people like you. They serve God in whatever way He asks them to serve Him, and that's always by sharing their talents, gifts, abilities, skill—and most of all, their love.

What do we live for if not to make the world less difficult for each other?
George Eliot

It Is What It Is

There's the proverbial elephant in the room—the reality we don't want to talk about. We hope that if we simply ignore it, the elephant might silently lumber out the door or disappear through the walls. But the elephant stays...and stays...and stays.

The longer we resist accepting a difficult fact, the larger it grows in our mind and the heavier it weighs in our thoughts. We wish it weren't true, but it is. We wish we could get rid of it, but we can't. We wish there were a quick fix, but there isn't. The only thing we can do is the hardest thing to do, and that's to call it what it is and accept it.

By accepting, we learn how to live in the real world—a world of grief and joy, loss and gain, heartbreaking circumstances and inspiring examples of heroism, courage, strength, and perseverance. Acceptance builds inner strength and self-confidence as we go forward, because we discover our ability to overcome and adapt as we reap the benefits of knowing how to face reality.

Those who are able to accept the elephant in the room often find to their relief and gratitude, that he has chosen, while they weren't looking, to vanish from their heart and mind.

Self-confidence is strengthened not by turning away from challenges but by facing them.

20/20 VISION

Several people can witness the same event, yet not see exactly the same thing. It's a phenomenon proven by studies that have asked participants to watch a video of a crime and then describe what happened. More often than not, each person will report the circumstances differently. Sometimes a viewer will notice what no one else did, and sometimes a person is certain about details that weren't even there!

The eyes we bring to our circumstances and the world around us determine what we're likely to notice, focus on, and remember. If our sight is shadowed by anger and bitterness, we'll see nothing but meanness, insults, and personal attacks as we interact with others. If we let resentment cloud our vision, we'll pick out every "reason" to feel slighted and unsatisfied. Yet with eyes of faith and gratitude, kindness and compassion, trust and optimism, we look out onto a world of good people, great opportunities, and priceless blessings.

What you see determines what you think, talk about, choose, and decide. The eyes of your heart and mind shape how you perceive other people and your relationships...what you remember about your past and what you expect in the future. There's no substitute for clear, healthy, wholesome, God-guided 20/20 vision.

Your vision is the promise of what you shall one day be.

James Allen

DRIVER'S ED

Who's in the driver's seat? When we really think about it, we're often startled to find that our life's driver is ambition...popularity... money...self-gratification. Sometimes we discover that we're merrily riding along with what other people think, say, and do. Or we're simply letting others determine our direction, regardless of where we would like to end up. The driver in charge of our life determines the route our life will take. Doesn't it make sense to know who's at the wheel?

Now you might think that you should grab the wheel yourself. But can you claim unerring knowledge of the path ahead? Can you foresee the road blocks and detours you might run into along the way, and know how to handle them? If you're driving solo, who will be able to guide you back to the right road when you realize you've taken a wrong turn-off and want to get back on the highway again?

The longer you travel on life's road, the more you'll discover that your all-knowing God is the only one you want in the driver's seat. He alone has the map of your life. He alone can take you to those places where you can best use your gifts and talents. He alone can clear the way to life's purpose and fulfillment.

**If God is your co-pilot,
swap seats!**

LOL!

Laughter is something most of us wait to come to us. When we're hanging out with a group of witty friends, we know they'll say things that will sweep us up in gales of laughter. When we tune in to our favorite comedy show or listen to a funny late-night host, we expect to hear jokes that will make us laugh out loud.

But what if there's no one around saying anything funny? That's when it's time to look for laughter. Really, it's everywhere! There's laughter in the dance of sunbeams skipping across rippling water and in the song of leaves skittering along the sidewalk...in the giggles of children at play and in the whimsy of clouds floating across the sky...in a delightfully surprising turn of events and in a wry observation overheard while waiting in the grocery check-out line.

Once you start looking for laughter, you'll see it in ordinary things, in ordinary places. In no time at all, you'll be the person who's pointing out the everyday funnies to others. You'll be the person friends especially love to meet, because you have a way of making them feel good. You know how to make them laugh!

Laughter lightens the heart.

Lookin' Good!

When we're young, we're often extremely self-critical. Somehow our "defects"—everything from an isolated pimple to an embarrassing case of stage fright—seem like a catastrophe in the making. But, believe it or not, there comes a time when we decide to like ourselves the way we are. No, it doesn't mean shutting ourselves off from a chance for growth or fine-tuning here and there; it's just that we're no longer fretting about that awkward moment or quirky personality trait that refuses to go away.

For most people, it takes decades to reach this level of self-acceptance. Then, if you could talk to your younger self, you'd say, "What were you waiting for? You're okay, and you were always okay!" So, Graduate, why not start now? Why not like yourself today?

You know how to encourage others, but you may not know to encourage yourself. Do it! When you see your friends looking great, you tell them, don't you? So when you look in the mirror and find you looking fabulous, compliment yourself! Stand up straight, hold your head high, and smile!

It's great to receive compliments from others, but it's wonderful to hear them once in a while from the person you're closest to—you. You deserve every single one!

**What you think about yourself
is much more important
than what others think of you.**
Seneca

Self-Portrait

When an interviewer asks you to describe
yourself, what kinds of words do you use?
Perhaps for the sake of modesty, you shy away
from saying anything very flattering. But in
truth, you have every reason to list dozens of
impressive traits and special gifts.

When you use affirmative, upbeat, and
positive words to describe who you are and
your skills and talents, you're doing more than
generating healthy self-esteem. Your self-as-
sessment and private feelings make themselves
known in the way you speak, dress, and act
around others. And how you present yourself
goes a long way in signaling how you expect
to be respected and treated by them.

Your inner self-opinions also affect the choices
you make. If you feel good about yourself, you
expect to get recognition for your efforts.

You assume you'll achieve and receive your earned rewards. Given options, you'll take the one that lifts your heart and mind, improves your situation, moves you forward, and works toward your ultimate good and the good of those around you.

Only on certain occasions you will be required to list your skills and describe your expertise; but every day you talk about them to yourself. The words you use are important...and they're impossible to hide.

If you want to be respected by others, the great thing is to respect yourself.
Fyodor Dostoyevsky

Pain Management

"Pain is inevitable," goes an old observation, "but suffering is optional." This time-tested truth points to the fact that pain and hardship—sometimes even intense pain and devastating hardship—enter our lives at certain points. Sometimes it's long-lasting, as when chronic illness is diagnosed and lengthy treatments required. Sometimes it's sudden and overwhelming, as when loss and misfortune blindside us, seemingly coming out of nowhere.

How you handle trouble is what separates those who manage downturns and those who let downturns manage them. If you let a bad situation get control, it draws you into prolonged suffering, despondency, and despair. It convinces you that there's nothing you can do, so you may as well curl up and suffer—and it's all too tempting to do just that. But when you manage trouble, you take all the necessary steps to lessen its hold on you. You believe in God's presence and His power...that means you believe you can successfully get through it or learn to live with it—and guess what? You do!

Resources to help you through any trouble you might be experiencing now or may experience in the future come from many places. There's encouragement, strength, wisdom, and understanding from family members, friends, mentors, counselors, medical professionals...and always from God.

Drag your thoughts away
from your troubles...
by the ears, by the heels,
or any other way you can manage it.
Mark Twain

Pray And...

"When all else fails, pray!" That's how some people react when trouble comes their way. But here's the question: Why deal with the frustration of failing? Other people see trouble looming on the horizon and immediately fall down on their knees as their first and only resort. Yet here's another question: Doesn't God enable and empower us to use what He has given us to solve our problems?

The fact is, it's pray *and...* Pray *and* open your eyes so you can see God's plan for you. Pray *and* get up on your feet so you can follow where He's leading you through the present situation. Pray *and* unfold your hands so you can work toward getting your issue solved by using the mental, emotional, and material resources He has given to you. While He gladly gives you the strength to move forward, He expects you to use His strength to meet the challenge in front of you.

Sure, God could, at the sound of your voice, miraculously remove your troubles, and occasionally He might do exactly that. Most of the time, however, you will find that He gives you everything you need when you ask Him. He invites you to pray *and* start taking action.

Work as if everything depended upon work, and pray as if everything depended upon prayer.

William Booth

HEAD OVER HEELS

Have you ever been head over heels in love
with someone? If so, you know how this
love turns your whole world brighter. Even
ordinary days sparkle with excitement! Head-
over-heels love opens hope for the future
and all the possibilities tomorrow could hold.
It sweeps away fear and discouragement because you know that no matter what comes,
you'll have each other.

When you're wildly in love, you're always
looking forward to your next chance to see
the one you love, and you treasure in your
heart all the times you share together. Talking
about the things your special one has said and
done brings pleasure, pride, and joy; simply
thinking about your beloved warms your
heart and makes you smile.

Love for God works in a similar way, and
that's why poets and writers, composers and

storytellers since ancient times have compared spiritual love to ideal romantic love. It's a way of helping us grasp what the human mind cannot comprehend, and that's the depth, breadth, and height of God's infinite, all-encompassing, unconditional love for each of us. It's a way to guide us along the path of spiritual love, a love that knows no end.

Don't be afraid to fall head over heels in love with Him, because He's already head over heels in love with you!

**Feel God's love surrounding you
and lifting you up
in every moment of every day.**
N. L. Roloff

HERE'S HOW

Why spend so many years in school? The answer's obvious: so you can learn from your teachers how to think critically, mature intellectually, and master the skills you need to build a fulfilling and productive future. Note that these things are not required of you before your teachers have taught you how!

Before asking us to serve others in down-to-earth, practical ways, God shows us how by serving each one of us in down-to-earth, practical ways. He does this through the example set by Jesus when He walked among us, healing, helping, and humbly serving the people He met. In the words of Scripture, God teaches us how to think, speak, and behave. Before we're asked to serve, we learn how from Him!

As lifelong students of God, we have the best teacher ever. Belief that God created us provides personal self-worth. Awareness of His presence wherever we are gives us courage and self-confidence. Acceptance of His Word as true and unchanging builds with us a firm foundation and an unfailing standard in matters of faith, morality, and conduct. Reliance on the power of prayer reminds us that God is the source of our help and strength, our comfort and peace of mind.

Learn from Him, and serve others with confidence!

The best sermon is a good example.

PASSWORD PROTECTION

What's your password? You know not to blurt out the combination of letters, numbers, and symbols that guards your private accounts. Even so, as a prudent and savvy Internet user, you constantly keep a watchful eye out so your information doesn't slip into the wrong hands.

Even more worth guarding is your connection with God. It's what keeps you spiritually alive and energized, growing and productive, purposeful and motivated to follow His promptings and guidelines. Your relationship with God is what revives you when you're feeling down and renews you when you find that you're completely out of power. When you turn over to God the worry that is stirring in you, a sadness that is on your heart, or a concern that's on your mind, it's a way of reminding yourself that you are not alone. It's a connection to calm the heart, and carry on with confidence.

It's what provides you with the information you need to make good decisions, and to remain faithful to God.

Fortunately, the password is easy to remember. It's PRAYER.

PRAYER...
your direct line to God.

KNOW WHAT?

No matter how far we've been or plan to go in school, there will always be people who know more than we do. It's hard for some of us to admit sometimes, but true. And if we're smart (or aspire to smartness), we'll listen to them. That's because, no matter how impressive our intellect or lofty our academic degree, there's no one human being who knows it all.

The only one who knows everything is God—or He wouldn't be God, would He? He definitely deserves a listen, because He knows what He's talking about! Your willingness to hear Him speak in the words of Scripture shows that you acknowledge His timeless and time-tested wisdom and authority. Your sensitivity to the voice of your conscience reveals your readiness to obey God's rules and guidelines. Your eagerness to learn from the advice and example of mature Christians displays your desire to remain teachable and to grow in knowledge.

Be generous with what you know, because you can help others out who are willing to learn from you. At the same time, listen to those who can help you with their knowledge and expertise. But even more importantly, listen to God, who really and truly knows it all.

People who accomplish things that count are usually too busy to count their accomplishments.

Play Nice

If you have learned to play a musical instrument or trained as a dancer, gymnast, or athlete, you know the importance of constant practice. Perhaps you even heard an instructor or coach offer these words of warning: Miss a day of practice, and you know it; miss two days, and your teacher knows it; miss three days, and the audience knows it.

Kindness is like a musical instrument, and if we want to get good at it, we need to practice every day. When we're content to miss days here and there, we fall out of practice, leaving us with less desire to go back and start over.

As you go about your day, look for practice opportunities. They're all around you! Offer a warm smile and friendly greeting instead of a casual nod...ask to help before you're asked...

be thankful for little blessings and let your gratitude show...note what's working well, what's to feel good about, and tell someone rather than complain about what's not.

The whisper of conscience tells you when you've missed an opportunity to practice. A new day opens a chance to begin again.

Every day...
God gives us a chance to make a beautiful difference in the world.

Standing Ovation

How about those shenanigans you—or, ahem, *others*—pulled in school? Here's a classic:

A couple of college pranksters took it upon themselves to remove all the chairs from the auditorium one afternoon before the lecture of a noted professor. No one noticed until ticket holders began arriving for the event, and by that time it was too late to retrieve the chairs from wherever the students had stashed them, and arrange them in rows. So the audience had no choice but to stand throughout the professor's presentation. The next day, the professor told her friends about her evening. "It was fantastic," she enthused. "This was the best audience I've ever had! They gave me a standing ovation from the moment I entered the room!"

Things aren't always what they seem, but blessed are those who can put a positive spin on the situation! Your ability to laugh, and your readiness to look on the bright side, no matter what happens to you, helps you make the best of every situation. Today, give the world (and yourself) a standing ovation!

An optimist is a fisherman who, when he goes out fishing, takes along a camera and a frying pan.

Be Part Of The Action

Lots of things look easy—easy, that is, as long as we're sitting on the sidelines watching other people do them. When we're part of the action, however, we find complexities and challenges we never knew existed. Things don't look so easy anymore, and comments from the chair-sitters aren't improving our ability to cope.

It has been said that you cannot know another person's struggles without first walking a mile in their shoes. Perhaps they're out there facing huge obstacles, yet doing their best and giving it all they've got. Don't they deserve a pat on the back? Instead of comments and criticism from the peanut gallery, the helping hand of someone who's willing to get out there with them would be more than welcome. Even knowing that someone else cares enough to listen and learn about their reality can ease the burden they carry.

Before you weigh in with your advice and opinions, look beyond what's easy to see. Step outside your sphere of personal experience and try to understand the other person's experience and point of view. You don't have to agree; and perhaps you do know of a better way. But you won't be able to change anything for the better unless you become part of the action.

It's much more constructive to give someone a hand-up than a put-down.
N. L. ROLOFF

PICTURE THIS!

People respond to what they see. If you doubt it, just think of the impact a single video can have on public opinion, despite the many stories written on the same topic.

In the same way, talking about being a Christian doesn't have the same effect as living as one. People believe what they see. There are so many ways for them to see the true goodness in you...when you're observed treating others with kindness and respect; taking the path of what is the right thing to do instead of going along with what the crowd says; offering to help people in real and practical ways; being generous with your skills, talents, and resources; and taking time to listen to the concerns of others, to truly understand them and care about them. When you let your true light shine in ways like these, you create a visual story that's hard to ignore. The power of your words is far greater when backed by your actions.

And who knows? Imagine what it would be like if goodness went viral!

The recommended daily vitamin for Christians is B-1.

ORDER IN THE WORLD

"There's a method to my madness," you might assure anyone who asks. Your desk, your workspace, or even your whole living space might look chaotic, but you know what goes where. You know exactly what you plan to do and when you plan to do it.

If you listen to national and world news, it might seem as if chaos rules the world. Where there could be order and harmony, there's trouble, upset, and confusion.

People commit unthinkable acts. Natural disasters leave a trail of destruction. Sadness happens. It's hard to understand how such turn of events could possibly serve a higher good or bring about a positive outcome. If, however, we remember who created the world and who continues to control it, we perceive plan and purpose. We believe God remains in control of His creation.

From our vantage point, we can't always comprehend God's method, but He knows exactly what He plans to do, and when he plans to do it.

**Life is a learning process
designed by God
to teach us what we need to know.**
N. L. Roloff

A Happy Event

Imagine Happiness standing on your front porch, knocking and calling for you to open the door. Would you swing the door open? Would you invite her in as a welcome guest, to settle in and get comfortable? As it happens, a lot of people wouldn't. Excuses run the gamut from "I don't deserve to be happy" (downright wrong) to "I've got to be sad, miserable, depressed because God wants me to make up for mistakes I've made in the past" (double-downright wrong to the person who came up with that idea).

When it comes to happiness, many of us let fear of the unknown pull us back. While we may not like our situation, at least it's familiar. Even apathy can keep us away from answering the door to happiness. After all, pursuing happiness may call for some action on our part.

So, If you are stalling, what's your excuse? After you've shown your excuses the back door, swing the front door wide open for happiness!

Dare to live the life
you have dreamed for yourself.
Go forward and make
your dreams come true.
Ralph Waldo Emerson

THE FACE OF GOD

The eyes of God shine with love, and He looks with care and compassion on you. He keeps you in His sight, and He blesses you with all you need to fulfill His divine purpose for you. His generosity knows no end, and His goodwill extends to you at all times.

Close your eyes and see the beautiful face of God...and in it the faces of all those who know and love you.

Thou art greatly beloved.
Daniel 9:23